BIG BU$INE$$

Coca-Cola

Cath Senker

First published in 2012 by Wayland

Wayland
338 Euston Road
London NW1 3BH

Wayland Australia
Level 17/207 Kent Street
Sydney, NSW 2000

Managing editor: Debbie Foy
Designer: Emma Randall
Picture researcher: Shelley Noronha

Picture Acknowledgments: The author and publisher would like to thank the following for allowing their pictures to be reproduced in this publication: Cover image: Shutterstock; 4 source:www.rzuser.uni-heidelberg.de/~el6/presentations/pres_c2_hoa/CCSalesfigures 5 Ahmad Yusni/AFP/Getty Images; 6, 7 UPPA/Photoshot; 8 Bettman/Corbis; 9 The Coca Cola Company Hand Out/DPA/Corbis; 10 Picture Alliance/Photoshot; 11 Robert Maass/Corbis; 12 Gideon Mendel/In Pictures/Corbis; 13 Chris Graythen/Getty Images; 14 Getty images; Map source CNBC.com; 15 Caro/Alamy; 16 2005 ©Sean Sprague/The Image Works/TopFoto; 17 Raveendran/AFP/Getty Images; 18 Gideon Mendel/Corbis; 19 Greg Wood/AFP/Getty Images; 20 Bloomberg via Getty Images; 21 Infographic The Coca Cola Company; 22 STR/Reuters/Corbis; 23 Getty Images; 24 STR/AFP/Getty Images; 25 ©Jack Kurtz/ The Image Works/TopFoto; 26 Keystone/TopFoto.co.uk; 27 © Photoshot. Every attempt has been made to clear copyright for this edition. Should there be any inadvertent omission please apply to the publisher for rectification.

British Library Cataloguing in Publication Data:
Senker, Cath.
Coca Cola : the story behind the iconic business. -- (Big business)
1. Coca-Cola Company--Juvenile literature. 2. Soft drink industry--Juvenile literature.
I. Title II. Series III. Foy, Debbie.
338.7′66362-dc23

ISBN: 978 0 7502 6921 6

Printed in China
Wayland is a division of Hachette Children's Books, an Hachette UK company.
www.hachette.co.uk

Contents

Coca-Cola at the top

Have you ever grabbed an ice-cold Coke from the chiller cabinet on a hot day? If you have, you're in good company. Every day, 1.7 billion servings of Coca-Cola are consumed. That's equivalent to a drink each for a quarter of the world's population! Coca-Cola, made by the Coca-Cola Company (CCC), is the most popular soft drink in the world.

The Coca-Cola Company is a huge international company at its height and still expanding. With its headquarters in Atlanta, Georgia, it is one of the largest corporations in the USA. In 2012, it had 139,600 employees and sold more than 3,500 products in over 200 countries. This phenomenal success is based mostly on just one soft drink – Coca-Cola.

John Pemberton invented Coca-Cola in Atlanta in 1886. From its humble beginnings as a health drink sold in a small local chemist's shop, the product became the core of a giant business selling syrup to be bottled and distributed around the world. It also became a part of daily life in the USA and a symbol of American culture across the globe.

The main activity of the CCC remains the manufacture and sale of syrup for making Coca-Cola. Yet it also produces and sells a wide variety of other drinks – from Inca Kola, a sparkling drink in South America, to Vita, an African juice drink, and Samurai, an Asian energy drink.

This book will explore the history of the CCC, the far-sighted individuals who built the brand, its overwhelming success and also its setbacks. It will look at the vital aspects of the business such as innovation, marketing, packaging and sponsorship that have made the company what it is today.

This chart shows the amount of Coca-Cola servings sold by year.

	Selling Numbers of Coca-Cola
1886	9 glasses per day
1902	over 200 million
1907	over 1 billion
1910	over 2 billion
1914	over 4 billion
1919	over 10 billion
1936	over 100 billion
1952	over 200 billion
1958	over 300 billion
1965	over 500 billion
1973	over 1 trillion
1993	over 4 trillion
2003	over 6 trillion
2010	6.2 trillion

Business Matters

Biggest and best known – Coca-Cola is the biggest drinks manufacturer and distributor in the world. Studies have shown that Coca-Cola is one of the best-known trademarks. After the word 'OK,' Coca-Cola is the second most widely understood term by people across the globe. So you could be virtually anywhere in the world, ask for a Coke and be understood!

> "The curvy script, roll-off-the-tongue name, bright red colouring and iconic bottle shape have made Coca-Cola the most famous brand on the planet. . . . It's certainly the most easily recognised logo ever."
>
> ***James Wheatley, creative producer at Swamp market research agency***

▼ *A billboard advertising Coca-Cola in Kuala Lumpur, Malaysia.*

'A delicious and refreshing beverage'

When Atlanta chemist John S. Pemberton developed the beverage at the Pemberton Chemical Company, the drink contained cocaine from the coca leaf and caffeine-rich extracts from the kola nut. Cocaine is a strong drug that is illegal today; in fact, it was dropped from the Coca-Cola recipe in 1905. The kola nut comes from trees that grow in tropical African and American countries. (Nowadays, US and European soft-drink producers manufacture chemicals with a flavour similar to the kola nut.)

Pemberton served his product at Jacobs' Pharmacy as a health drink intended to cure common ailments. He claimed that Coca-Cola relieved headaches and was good for the brain and nerves. Once cocaine was no longer used, the company soon dropped the medical claims for the drink – although the caffeine in the drink still gave drinkers a 'buzz'. Yet the name Coca-Cola, based on the original cocaine ingredient, remained. It was Pemberton's bookkeeper Frank Robinson who had chosen the name and he wrote it in the script that became the Coca-Cola logo. This has changed little over the years.

A traditional glass Coca-Cola bottle with the trademark red Coca-Cola logo that dates back to 1893.

Calendars used to be a popular way to advertise Coca-Cola.

From the start, Pemberton used advertising to promote his new drink. His first advert in 1886 described his product as a 'Delicious and Refreshing Beverage'. He was soon selling his syrup to local pharmacies, which in those days had soda fountains – dispensers for fizzy drinks. Coca-Cola quickly gained popularity. But Pemberton decided to sell his growing business to another Atlanta pharmacist, Asa Griggs Candler.

Brains Behind The Brand

Asa Griggs Candler – founder of the Coca-Cola Company

Mr Candler owned a successful pharmacy business, making and selling drugs. From 1888 he began to take over the Coca-Cola business from Pemberton. He bought the Coke formula and secured the patent – the right to make the drink. By 1891 Candler had total ownership of Coca-Cola. He formed the Coca-Cola Company (CCC) in 1892 and registered the Coca-Cola name as a trademark in 1893. Candler then set about improving the process of manufacturing the beverage. The CCC rapidly became the most successful business in the US South. By 1895, the product was sold in every US state. Under Candler, sales soared from around 34,000 litres (9,000 US gallons) of syrup in 1890 to 1,403,922 litres (370,877 US gallons) in 1900.

Business Matters

Advertising – From the very beginning, the CCC cleverly used advertising to link Coke to the American lifestyle. Adverts showed Americans enjoying a Coke break as part of their daily life. in this way, Coke became connected with ordinary people enjoying a relaxing moment with friends or workmates – an image with wide appeal.

Coke and the American way of life

In 1899, with sales increasing, Candler found a cunning solution to expand production while keeping the formula for the Coca-Cola syrup top secret to protect the brand.

Candler sold the rights to bottle Coca-Cola in most of the USA to a bottling company owned by Benjamin F. Thomas and Joseph B. Whitehead in Chattanooga, Tennessee. Thomas and Whitehead were allowed to buy the syrup, add water, bottle and distribute the drink. Selling the rights to bottle Coca-Cola allowed the company to greatly widen distribution. In 1906, the company also established bottling operations outside the USA, in Canada, Cuba and Panama. The 'Coca-Cola system' was so successful that it was adopted by other US drinks producers.

US soldiers on the front line in Italy in 1944 gulp down Coke on the battlefield.

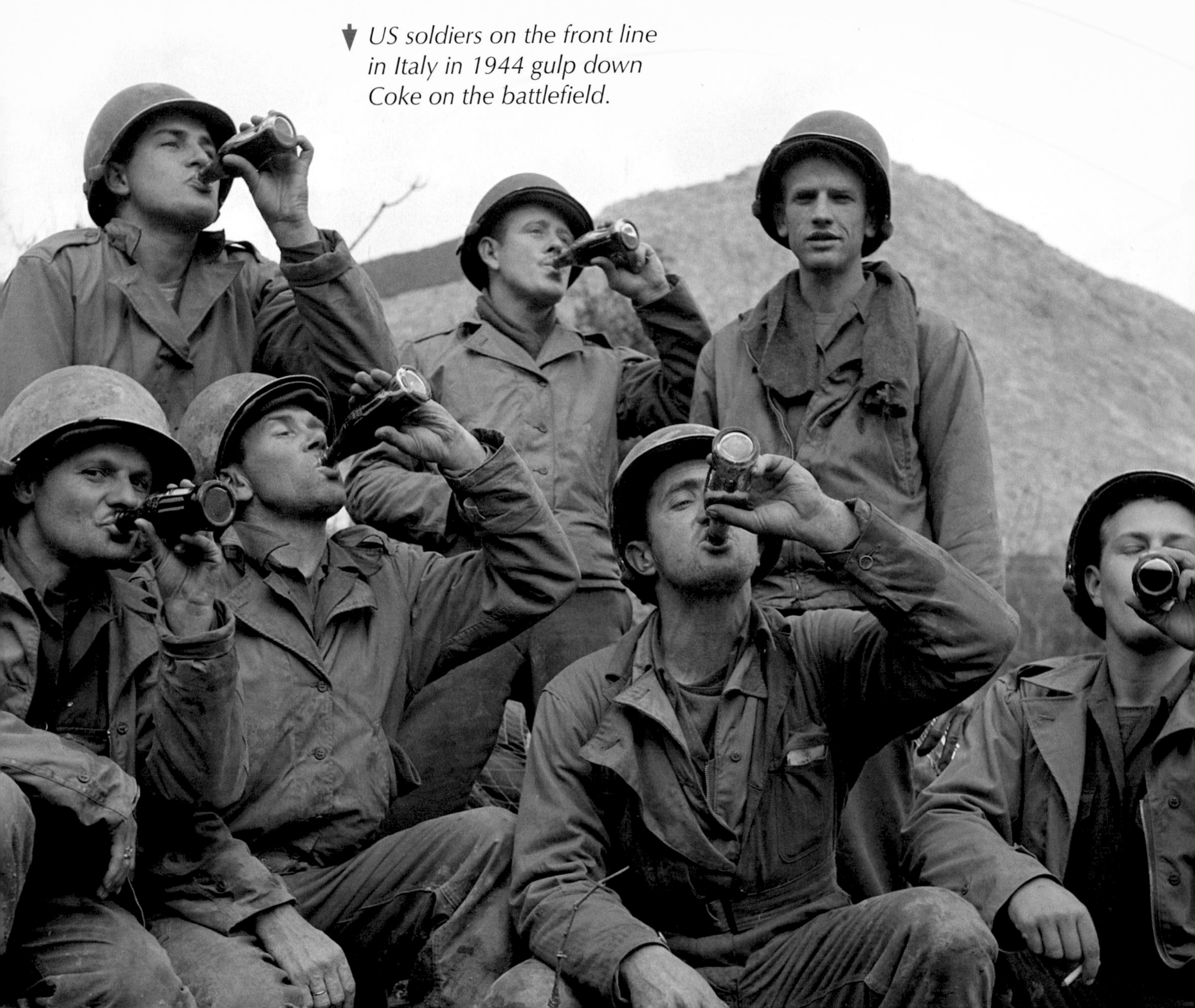

A cheery Santa created by Haddon Sundblom advertises Coca-Cola in the 1930s. Note how the red of Santa's jacket closely matches that of the company's logo.

Marketing was also crucial to the company's startling success. Brand recognition was established through the design of the Coke bottle. The distinctive bottle shape was produced in 1916 and remains the most recognized bottle in the world today!

In 1919, the company changed hands again. A group of investors led by Atlanta businessman Ernest Woodruff bought the company. Ernest's son Robert Winship Woodruff was president and chairman of the company from 1923–55. The Woodruffs undertook massive advertising campaigns. For example, in 1921 the 'Thirst Knows No Season' slogan was introduced, to encourage people to drink Coca-Cola all year round, not just in summer. The campaign continued with adverts that connected Coca-Cola with Santa Claus. The company's advertising was necessary to stay ahead of the game. In the 1930s, there was growing competition from Pepsi, which produced a similar product – but cheaper.

The CCC found a new opportunity to embed itself in the American way of life during World War II. In 1943, US military leaders agreed that providing Coke to the soldiers could boost their morale and encourage them to drink less alcohol. Woodruff declared Coca-Cola's wartime policy: 'We will see that every man in uniform gets a bottle of Coca-Cola for five cents wherever he is and whatever it costs.' Portable bottling plants were sent to Asia, Europe and North Africa, and Coca-Cola became part of the US war effort.

Business Matters

Marketing – Did you know that Santa wasn't always red, fat and jolly? He used to be a variety of shapes, sizes and colours. in 1931, after Coca-Cola had linked its advertising campaigns with Santa Claus, the company employed illustrator Haddon Sundblom to design a warm, friendly red Santa. in Coca-Cola adverts, Santa was shown delivering toys, playing with children and, of course, drinking Coke. The adverts appeared in magazines, shop displays, calendars and on billboards. This shrewd move helped to link Coke with the joy of Christmas.

New-look Coke – the 'real thing'

After World War II, the CCC expanded further. The company grew by buying other products, and introduced novel packaging and a brand-new look for Coke.

Marketing remained a top priority. As soon as television started broadcasting, the CCC was advertising on the small screen. Its first TV commercial appeared in 1950. In the 1950s, US advertisers rarely showed black people. Unusually, Coca-Cola began to feature African-Americans in its marketing. Of course, it made sense because it meant African-Americans were more likely to buy Coke.

In 1969, the company brought in a new look, with the red and white colour scheme and logo. The now-famous slogan 'It's the Real Thing' was introduced. Several Coca-Cola adverts became particularly iconic, such as 'I'd like to buy the world a Coke' (see page 11). Designed to appeal to young people, the 'Mean Joe' Greene commercial in 1979 featured the well-known American footballer throwing his jumper to a child in the stadium.

Companies need to diversify (move into different areas) to survive, and the CCC was no exception. It could not rely on the popularity of Coca-Cola alone, so it bought up other soft drinks: Fanta in 1946, Sprite (1961) and Tab in 1963. The company also entered the citrus-juice market, purchasing the Minute Maid Corporation in 1960 and Fresca in 1966.

Here you can see how the Coke bottle has changed its shape and size over time.

1899–1902 | 1900–1916 | 1915 | 1957 | 1961 | 1991 | 1993 | 2007

This billboard refers to the song 'I'd like to teach the world to sing' that was the basis for the 'Buy the world a Coke' advert.

Brains Behind The Brand

Bill Backer – Creative Director
In 1971, Bill Backer, the Creative Director for marketing company McCann Erickson, was working on the Coke campaigns. One wintry January day, Mr Backer's flight to the UK was delayed, and the plane was forced to land in Ireland, greatly annoying the passengers. At Shannon Airport the following morning, he spotted those passengers chatting over bottles of Coke. This gave him the idea for the advert: 'I began to see the familiar words, "Let's have a Coke," as a subtle way of saying, "Let's keep each other company for a little while."' Backer came up with the advert 'I'd like to buy the world a Coke'. Although the advert failed on the radio at first, when it was released on TV in the USA, it was a big hit. It is now seen as one of the best TV commercials of all time.

Business Matters

Packaging – The packaging of Coca-Cola altered over time to reflect changes in technology.

- 1915: the classic glass Coke bottle appeared. After drinking, the bottles were returned to the shop to be reused.
- 1960: steel cans were introduced to make the packaging less breakable and the product easier to transport.
- 1968: the non-returnable glass contour bottle was introduced.
- 1978: the company brought in PET recyclable plastic bottles. It was now up to the consumer to ensure the bottle was recycled.

Coke and sports

The Coca-Cola Company sponsors sports events and the entertainment industry. It provides money for events, in exchange for the right to advertise at them. Why does it do this?

Sponsorship is a great way for a company to raise its profile – everyone who watches the matches sees its adverts and logos. It is good for the company to link itself to healthy activities, promoting the idea that having a Coca-Cola helps you to enjoy the game. The brand is also publicized in the local area where the event takes place.

Coca-Cola began its association with sport when chairman Robert Woodruff set up kiosks outside the Olympic Games in Amsterdam, Holland in 1928. It introduced the Olympics into its advertising at the 1932 Los Angeles Games. Coca-Cola was present when the Olympics were held in Nazi Germany in 1936 (although the company would probably rather forget

An urban wall mural with runners against a background of Coke bubbles. It was launched by Coca-Cola to publicize the London Olympics in 2012.

this chapter in its history.) Over time, the CCC's activities at the Olympics developed; the kiosks were replaced by trading centres selling drinks. In 1992, it first sponsored the Olympic Torch Relay, generating excitement in the run-up to the Games.

In the early 21st century, the CCC was the exclusive non-alcoholic beverage provider for the Olympic Games – that is, the only company allowed to sell soft drinks at the Olympics. The CCC began advertising at FIFA World Cup matches in the 1950s. In 1976 it forged the first-ever sponsorship deal between a sports association and a company. The deal has been renewed ever since. According to the 2007–22 deal, the CCC agrees to sponsor all FIFA tournaments, including the FIFA World Cup, Women's World Cup and the World Youth Championship. It provides cash, products and services to support the FIFA events. In return, the company runs a global marketing campaign linking itself to World Cup football, with TV commercials, a music anthem, online advertising and commemorative packaging. And naturally, it sells its products to refresh the spectators at matches.

Coca-Cola sponsors other sports too, including the Tour de France cycle race, basketball and stock-car racing. In 1998, the CCC announced a 100-year partnership with National Basketball Association – a long-term deal indeed!

The company is also involved in the entertainment industry, sponsoring the US TV talent show *American Idol,* Apple iTunes and the BET (Black Entertainment Television) Network. By taking part in such a variety of industries, the company ensures its message reaches mass audiences.

Coca-Cola sponsors NASCAR stock-car racing in the USA.

"We're focused on building long term category plans with our customers to grow soft drink sales in Great Britain. We know that our sponsorship for London [Olympics] 2012 will energise this work."

Simon Baldry, Managing Director, Coca-Cola Enterprises Ltd

New markets, new drinks

The 1980s brought a new winner for Coca-Cola – Diet Coke. It also brought great business opportunities in Eastern Europe. By 2000, the company had increased its range of drinks to cater for sports enthusiasts and the health conscious as well as regular Coke drinkers.

In 1985, the CCC began bottling operations in Russia and it started selling Coca-Cola in East Germany in 1990. When Communism fell in Russia and Eastern Europe in 1989–91, the people were eager to sample Western products. Coca-Cola was a powerful symbol of life in the West and proved enormously popular. Another new market was India: Coca-Cola India was set up as a subsidiary of the CCC (a company controlled by the CCC) in 1993 and established bottling operations.

The low-calorie, sugar-free Diet Coke was introduced in 1982 to great fanfare. Although Pepsi had brought in its own diet version back in 1964, Diet Coke beat the competition and became the most popular low-calorie soft drink worldwide.

The labelled countries are the only ones where Coca-Cola is not sold.

An advert for Coca-Cola in Moscow, Russia in 1997

A worker on the assembly line at a Coke bottling plant in Poland.

> "All of the time and money and skill poured into consumer research on the new Coca-Cola could not measure or reveal the deep and abiding emotional attachment to original Coca-Cola."
>
> **Donald R Keough, Coke's president and chief operating officer, 1985**

Not all new developments were so successful. In 1985, the flavour of Coca-Cola was changed for the first time in its history. This updated version was called 'New Coke'. It was a disaster! The consumers hated it and caused a big outcry. Just 79 days later, the CCC revived the original flavour, marketed as Coca-Cola Classic. The company had acted quickly to respond to customers, admit its mistake and restore the original, well-loved formula.

The CCC's plan to diversify its drinks for different markets was better thought out. Powerade sports drink, launched in 1992, was named the official sports beverage of the Olympic Games, while Dasani bottled water (1999) was targeted at the health drinks market. Children's fruit drink Qoo was marketed in Asia from 1999. During the 1990s, the CCC bought up other brands to increase its market share further, acquiring Maaza, Thums Up and Limca in India; Barq's root beer in the USA; and Inca Kola in Peru. You could buy a CCC drink virtually anywhere in the world!

Brains Behind The Brand

Roberto Goizueta – Chairman and CEO

Born to a wealthy family in Cuba in 1931, Roberto Goizueta improved his English by watching American movies over and over again. After earning a degree in chemical engineering at Yale University, USA, he answered a Coca-Cola job advert for a chemical engineer in Havana, Cuba and was taken on. In 1960, after the Communists took power in Cuba, he left for the USA. Within CCC, Goizueta worked his way up from technical operations and eventually became Chairman and CEO in 1981. Goizueta devised the successful 'Coke is it' slogan and developed Diet Coke, one of the most popular new products of the 1980s.

Coca-Cola controversies

No company is perfect, but the CCC has been criticized for some extremely damaging practices, including human rights abuses, over-use of water and water pollution.

At Coca-Cola's bottling plant in Carepa, Colombia in the 1990s, members of the trade union Sinaltrainal accused the company of involvement in killing their members. The trade unionists argued that the managers of the factory opposed the trade union because it fought for higher wages. They believed the managers had contacted paramilitaries (an unofficial armed group) and asked them to attack the trade union leaders. Several were murdered; other members were terrified and left the union. The managers then introduced a pay cut. Yet the CCC did not accept any responsibility for the actions of the Colombian bottling plant. The trade union took the company to court in the USA in the early 2000s, but lost the case.

An anti-Coca-Cola poster from Colombia. It says, 'Don't drink Coca-Cola because it finances the war'.

Women from Benares, Uttar Pradesh, in India, protest in 2006 to demand the closure of a Coca-Cola bottling plant. They believe the factory has polluted their water supply.

Another issue is water use. In Nejapa, El Salvador in the early 2000s, a Coca-Cola bottling factory used up water from a stream that local people needed for drinking and washing. It dumped waste in the water, the fish died, and the water became too polluted to use. The Nejapa community had to bring in water tanks, and people had to pay for their water.

The Coca-Cola bottling plant in Mehdiganj, Varanasi, India has caused water shortages too. For example, in 2009 a drought hit the region, and the people of Mehdiganj, mostly farmers, struggled to find enough water for their basic needs and to water their crops. Yet the CCC continued to extract millions of litres of water for its bottling plant.

The CCC has responded to its critics. It has adopted a water stewardship plan, which aims to reduce the water used in production, recycle water used in manufacturing and support projects to restore the water supply in communities where it works. For example, in 2009, the company announced a project to provide clean water and sanitation to at least six million Africans by 2015.

“In complete disregard for the communities in which it operates, Coca-Cola has continued to extract millions of liters of water from the common groundwater resource [water supply under the ground] even as the community has been struggling to meet its basic water needs, including water for farming, our primary source of livelihood. And in a particularly brutal practice, Coca-Cola reaches its maximum water use in the summer months – exactly when the water shortages to the community are most acute.”

India Resource Center campaign bulletin calls for a protest against Coca-Cola in Mehdiganj, Varanasi, India, 2009

Coca-Cola: a marketing miracle

The CCC has extraordinary media power. It has seen off the competition and dealt with criticisms of its products. With its enormous advertising budget, the company successfully presents Coca-Cola in a positive light.

Since the late 19th century, Pepsi has produced a similar cola product. In 1975, Pepsi launched the 'Pepsi challenge' to counter the dominance of Coca-Cola. It invited consumers to test the taste of Pepsi and Coca-Cola. The media called the competition 'the cola wars'. Pepsi claimed that the results showed that consumers preferred the Pepsi taste, and the company's sales increased. However, Coca-Cola continued to outsell its rival.

The CCC has also tackled criticism of Coke for causing health problems. For example, Mexico is a major market for Coca-Cola: Mexicans drink more Coca-Cola per head of the population than any other nation! The country has seen a rapid rise in the consumption of soft drinks and the number of overweight people. Yet the CCC argues it is poor diet and a lack of exercise that cause the weight problems rather than simply drinking Coke.

A Coca-Cola 'Northern Lights' advert from 1993. The animated TV advert featuring polar bears became world-famous.

A billboard in Sydney, Australia with a traditional Coca-Cola advertising message.

The company also contends that it offers plenty of sugar-free, low-calorie alternatives. Yet there are health concerns about diet drinks, too. For instance, instead of sugar they contain a sweetener called aspartame. Some people argue that it can cause headaches, weight gain and serious problems such as epilepsy and brain tumours. However, public health organizations in many countries have investigated aspartame and found it safe to consume.

Coca-Cola succeeds in fending off health criticisms and promotes its products to an ever-wider audience. It focuses on cross-media campaigns that include adverts in the cinema, newspapers and magazines, and on TV, radio, billboards, Internet banners, YouTube videos and Google space. Marketing experts believe that cross-media campaigns have a bigger impact on purchasing decisions than one single medium alone. The Internet is particularly important because it allows fans to spread the word themselves. For example, Coke set up a Facebook page in 2008 featuring people's stories from around the world. It had over 42.7 million 'likes' by June 2012!

Business Matters

Wendy Clark – Senior Vice President, Marketing.

Wendy Clark believes Coca-Cola should keep traditional features in its marketing campaigns but also adopt novel themes to appeal to young people. For example, in 2010, during the FIFA World Cup in South Africa, the company used the song 'Wavin' Flag' by well-known Somali rapper K'naan in its adverts. Wendy firmly believes mobile marketing will prove the best way to reach customers. It's vital to test out new ideas. She notes, 'We've got bets placed in [a lot of places] . . . some of them won't work. That's how we're going to learn mobile.'

The challenge of sustainability

At the start of the 21st century, it was clear that people worldwide needed to tackle big environmental issues, including the overuse of resources and waste. Like other businesses, the CCC considered how to increase sales while making its products more sustainable.

Ever hungry for a bigger market share, in 2001, the CCC and international food giant Nestlé created Beverage Partners Worldwide to market ready-to-serve coffee and tea drinks, such as the iced tea, Nestea. In 2007, Coca-Cola acquired Energy Brands, Inc., which makes various enhanced waters (waters with added benefits such as vitamins). The CCC continued to innovate too, bringing out Coke Zero in 2005 – the Coca-Cola taste with no calories. Innovation was also urgently needed to make the company more sustainable. In 2009, the company proudly announced the introduction of PlantBottle PET packaging, made with up to 30 per cent plant-based materials. These are renewable resources, using sugar cane and

Workers sort plastic bottles at a recycling plant in Mexico run by a Coca-Cola bottling company.

This infographic shows how much recycled material is used in each type of bottle. All the bottles are 100% recyclable.

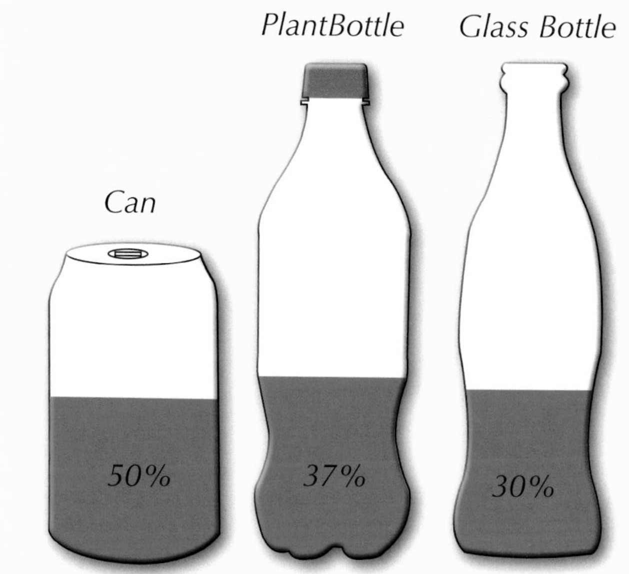

molasses (by-products of sugar production), and the bottles are completely recyclable. In 2011, rival Pepsi announced it would be bringing in the world's first PET plastic bottle made entirely from plant-based materials the following year. Such moves by major companies could reduce unnecessary waste from plastic bottles – as long as people remember to recycle them.

Another development was the 100 per cent recyclable display rack for Coca-Cola, introduced in 2011. Instead of placing Coke on their shelves, grocery shops can use this free-standing unit, made from recyclable cardboard. When customers see the unit, they'll link Coca-Cola with recycling in their minds – a clever piece of marketing as well as a useful innovation.

Brains Behind The Brand

Shell Huang – Director of Packaging Research

Shell Huang is personally committed to helping the environment. She drives a hybrid car (partly run on electricity rather than petrol alone) and her family always recycles. At work, she is determined to make the CCC's products more sustainable. Shell helped to invent the PlantBottle, which her team produces. The bottle is 100 per cent recyclable but not biodegradable (it doesn't break down into harmless substances in the earth). It is designed to be reused rather than thrown away. Huang's team is working on improving the design. She states, 'Our ultimate vision is to develop recyclable plastic bottles made from 100 per cent renewable materials.'

> "By creating a 100% recyclable merchandise display rack, Coca-Cola is asking grocery and convenience stores to join our sustainability efforts by returning or recycling our racks, just like we ask consumers to return our product packaging."

Gary Wygant, vice president of business development for Coca-Cola's recycling unit

Corporate social responsibility (CSR)

So what is corporate social responsibility? It means that a company takes responsibility for its own actions and tries to have a positive impact on society and the environment. How does the CCC measure up?

Coca-Cola has introduced CSR projects around the world. For instance, in 2010, a devastating earthquake hit Haiti. The people of this already poverty-stricken country found it harder than ever to make a living. The CCC launched the Haiti Hope Project. It was to give around US $7.5 million (£4.7 million) over five years to a project to help 25,000 mango farmers to develop a sustainable mango-juice industry. It was hoped the project would double the farmers' incomes.

In China, Coca-Cola works to protect the water supply. The company has 39 bottling plants along the heavily polluted Yangtze River. It is working to develop good water management policies. The CCC has also joined with the World Wildlife Fund to try to improve the water quality. For example, it is working with farmers to persuade them to use pig waste to produce bio-gas energy rather than dump it in the Yangtze river.

The relief effort in Haiti following the earthquake. Coca-Cola's Haiti Hope Project aimed to help farmers in the longer term.

Workers place Coca-Cola bottles into crates ready for distribution. Around 85 per cent of Coca-Cola's products in India and around the world are delivered in recyclable bottles and cans.

The CCC has adopted several CSR projects in India. It launched rainwater harvesting projects in Rajasthan, Varanasi and the city of Jamshedpur in 2006 and 2007. The rainwater is collected and returned to the groundwater supply. The company also aims to treat waste water from manufacturing effectively and return it to the environment.

The CCC has spent millions of dollars on a scheme to make its packaging sustainable by reducing the amount used, and recovering and reusing packaging after use. From 2005, the CCC established PET recycling projects around India and employed waste collectors to collect packaging materials from consumers for recycling.

Business Matters

'Greenwashing' – Not everyone agrees that Coca-Cola is helping people and the environment. Critics of Coca-Cola's CSR policies argue that the company is trying to give itself a green image, while continuing to damage the environment. They call this 'greenwashing'. For example, in India, local communities have continued to demonstrate against Coca-Cola for causing water shortages (see page 17). They say that the rainwater harvesting projects do not make up for all the water the company takes. The factories use up the groundwater in areas around them, so that farmers do not have enough water for their crops. The India Resource Center (which campaigns against the dominance of large international companies) has also claimed that the company allowed toxic waste water to flow into farmers' fields near the bottling plants. So is the company doing the best it can or is it engaged in greenwashing?

Muhtar Kent, head of Coca-Cola

Born in New York, the son of Turkish diplomats, Muhtar Kent went to school in England and travelled around the world before moving to the USA. In 1978, he was reading a newspaper in New York when he noticed an advert for a delivery-truck driver for Coca-Cola. It was an entry-level job, involving a lot of travel and hard work. But he knew the company's products and that it had a good reputation.

Luckily for Muhtar, he got the job. He travelled throughout the USA and learnt everything he could about sales, distribution and business operations (the activities involved in running the business), from the ground up. Muhtar gradually rose through the ranks in marketing and operations roles. He managed divisions of the company across the globe, including Coca-Cola Turkey and Central Asia, and a broad region that included Russia, China and Japan.

Muhtar Kent samples the beverages at a Coca-Cola technology centre in Shanghai, China.

Women drink Coke after a church service in Chiapa, Mexico. For rural people on very low incomes, bottled drinks are a rare treat.

Muhtar eventually reached the top of the company, becoming the CEO in 2008 and chairman the following year.

As the leader of an international company, Muhtar Kent puts all of the company's decisions through a 'global filter'. If someone comes up with a brilliant idea for Poland, he wonders: how would that go down in North America? Yet he's also keen to grow the business in the home of Coca-Cola. The USA has a rising population, the people are innovative and it's a good place for businesses to grow – including the many shops, bars and restaurants that sell Coca-Cola and its range of products.

Muhtar has additional challenges. The soft drinks industry has been criticized for contributing to obesity (when people are extremely overweight), for example, in the USA and Mexico. Muhtar defends the CCC from these accusations. He notes that the company has reduced the calorie content of many drinks and that it provides choice to consumers with its vast range of drinks. He believes absolutely in the business, commenting, 'I'm selling moments of pleasure at cents at a time billions of times a day.'

Business Matters

Staff development – The CCC has a staff development programme that takes 'rising stars' – talented young staff members – from across the company and sends them to special posts around the world. For example, a market researcher in the USA could be tasked with developing a juice strategy for Eurasia (Europe and Asia). Putting people out of their comfort zone allows them to learn new skills and helps to develop new leaders for the business.

"For our fans and our customers, choice is good – and we deliver... Sparkling and still... Calorie, mid-calorie, non-calorie... Juices, teas, coffees, sports drinks and many more."

Muhtar Kent, CEO, 16 November 2011

'2020 Vision': Coca-Cola's future

'2020 Vision' is the CCC's ambitious plan to double its business between 2010 and 2020 while becoming more sustainable.

On the sustainability front, the CCC is installing hydrogen fuel cells to power equipment such as forklift trucks, which can reduce energy use in its factories by 30 to 35 per cent. The company aims to achieve water neutrality (replacing as much water as it uses) by 2020, by using less water, recycling more, and rainwater harvesting.

Can the CCC double its business? The company believes that as an increasing number of people move to cities, there will be a greater demand for drinks on the go. One of the company's major growing markets is China, where Coca-Cola's juice beverages are extremely popular.

A Coke production plant in Berlin, Germany. The use of hydrogen fuel cells to power equipment could be extended from the USA to other countries in the future.

To spread its message, Coca-Cola will use the latest media and information technologies. For example here's its strategy for social media marketing:

- Reviewing: Marketing people check out the chatter about Coca-Cola, for example, on the Coca-Cola Conversation blog.
- Responding: They blog to answer questions or comment on the chatter.
- Recording: They produce content that's informative and helpful to social media users.
- Redirecting: They direct web traffic back to the Coca-Cola website.

The plan is to use technology to connect with consumers, allowing them to contribute their ideas. The company tells 'brand stories' about a product, such as 'real taste, zero sugar' to describe Coke Zero. These provoke comments from consumers; the company responds and has an online conversation with them. This way, Coca-Cola makes personal links with its fans and receives valuable feedback.

Clearly, the CCC will remain at the forefront of innovation in marketing, and is likely to stay the number-one soft-drinks company in the world.

Brains Behind The Brand

Designers – producing the vending machine of the future

Pininfarina, the Italian company that makes Ferraris, designed the Coca-Cola Freestyle machine. This fountain dispenser offers more than 100 drinks, including sparkling, low-calorie, sports drinks and flavoured waters. Its touch screen means consumers can mix their own drink at the touch of a button. Linked to the Internet, the machine collects data about the drinks served so the CCC can see which are the most popular choices.

The Coca-Cola Freestyle soft drinks machine, was introduced in 2011.

Design your own Coca-Cola venture

To create a new product, it is useful to put together a product development brief like the one below. This is a sample brief for Coca-Cola Ice Cream.

The SWOT analysis on the page opposite can help you to think about the strengths and weaknesses of your products, and the opportunities and threats presented. Then you can see how practical your idea is before you think of investing in it.

Product Development Brief

Name of product: Coca-Cola Ice Cream

Type of product: Ice Cream

The product explained (use 25 words or less): Coca-Cola ice cream brings customers the classic Coke taste in a refreshing ice cream – also available in low-fat and low-sugar options.

Target age of consumers: All ages.

What is the product? It is a classic, dairy-based ice cream with Coca-Cola flavouring.

Are there any similar products available? None that I know of.

What makes your product different? There are many cola drinks but no cola ice creams.

SWOT Analysis (Strengths, Weaknesses, Opportunities and Threats)

Name of Coca-Cola venture you are assessing . . . Coca-Cola Ice-Cream. The information below will help you assess the venture. By addressing all four areas, you can make your venture stronger and more likely to be a success.

Questions to consider	***Strengths***
What is unique and innovative about it?	***There is no other ice cream like it. It has never been produced commercially.***
What are its USPs? (unique selling points)	***It contains healthy ingredients such as milk and eggs combined with the unique Coke taste.***
Why will people buy this ice-cream rather than another kind?	***The Coca-Cola taste is well loved and the strength of the brand will encourage people to buy it.***
	Weaknesses
Why wouldn't people buy it?	***They may prefer to buy better-known brands.***
Does it live up to the claims you make?	***The product will be produced in low-fat, low-sugar versions, but is still less healthy than alternatives such as frozen yogurt.***
Are the potential losses worth risking the investment needed to develop the product?	***Coca-Cola is an expanding and profitable company but if the product fails, it could damage its reputation for a while, as New Coke did in 1980s.***
	Opportunities
Could the range of products offered expand in the future?	***Yes. If successful, a variety of Coke-flavoured ice creams could be made.***
Could it be sold globally?	***Yes. The global market for ice cream is growing, with new markets such as China and India.***
Can it develop new USPs?	***New products could be developed, depending on consumer preferences.***
	Threats
Will Coca-Cola ice cream face too much competition from other ice creams?	***Coca-Cola may not be able to compete with the big players in the industry, such as Unilever and Nestlé.***
Are any of the weaknesses so bad that they might affect the success of the venture in the long term?	***There are no obvious weaknesses that would affect the long-term success of the venture.***

Do you have the skills the company needs? Try this quiz!

The CCC employs people in a wide range of jobs, including business management, logistics, manufacturing, marketing, IT, finance and innovation.

1. You're choosing a soft drink and...
a) You grab your favourite brand as soon as you spot it.
b) You realize that within seconds the drinks bottle will become rubbish to dispose of.
c) You notice the packaging and wonder if it could be made lighter and use more renewable resources.

2. As you're drinking an ice-cold soft drink on a hot day, what are you thinking?
a) Nothing – you're just enjoying the moment.
b) You're enjoying the drink and comparing it to other similar products.
c) You wonder why soft drinks companies are so successful at marketing their products – you have lots of ideas for adverts yourself.

3. Your family has friends coming over. What do you do?
a) Keep out of the way until they arrive.
b) Help make the food and drink.
c) Take charge of making refreshments for the children – it's a great chance to try out your ideas for delicious mixed-fruit drinks.

4. Your class wants to fundraise for a charity at school. What do you do?
a) Wait for someone to come up with a good idea.
b) Do the same activity as last year – it seemed to go fine.
c) Find out which fundraising activities were most successful last year and do something better.

5. Your sports club is holding an event. How do you publicize it?
a) You tell your friends and family.
b) You put up posters at school.
c) You put up posters at school, ask permission to put up posters in local shops and ask a parent to help you send details to the local media.

6. You have several pieces of homework to do but it's your best friend's birthday. What do you do?
a) Skip the homework and go straight to your friend's house.
b) Do the quickest, easiest piece of homework and then go to the birthday celebrations.
c) Do the homework that needs to be done first and plan when you're going to fit in the other pieces. Then off to the party!

Results

Mostly As: You don't seem to be thinking about how to build up skills for your future career. Why not think about your strengths and see if you could contribute more at school or during activities you attend?

Mostly Bs: You are starting to learn some useful skills that will help in a future job. See if you can develop these further at school or through other activities.

Mostly Cs: You already have some skills that would be valuable to a company like Coca-Cola. Keep working on them at school and through your other activities, and maybe one day you'll work for a soft drinks company!

Glossary

beverage A drink, especially one other than water.

bio-gas energy Energy produced from waste matter from living creatures.

brand A product made by a particular company under a particular name.

by-product A secondary product made during the production of something else.

commemorative Intended to help people to remember an important event.

commercial The US word for 'advertisement'.

consumer A person who buys goods or services.

corporation A large business company.

cross-media campaign A marketing campaign that uses different kinds of media, for example, TV, posters, the Internet and mobile phones.

distributor A company that supplies goods to shops.

diversify For a company to develop a wider range of products to increase profits and reduce risk.

groundwater Water that is found under the ground, for example, in soil and rocks.

headquarters The place from which an organization controls its work.

human rights abuse Failing to respect people's basic human rights, for example, the right to live in freedom or organizations such as trade unions.

hydrogen fuel cell A fuel cell that converts the gas hydrogen into electricity.

iconic Acting as a sign or symbol of something.

innovation A new method, idea or product.

logo A symbol adopted by an organization to identify its products.

marketing Promoting and selling goods or services, including advertising and market research (finding out about what customers want).

non-returnable A container that cannot be returned to the manufacturer to be reused.

patent The official right to be the only company or individual to make, use or sell a product.

PET A safe plastic used for drink containers.

recyclable Able to be recycled.

renewable resource A resource that can be renewed naturally over time, for example, plant products or wood.

sanitation The system that keeps places clean, especially by removing human waste.

slogan A word or phrase that is easy to remember, used by advertisers to attract people's attention.

sponsorship When a company gives money for a sporting or entertainment event, in return for permission to advertise at the event.

subsidiary company A company that is controlled by another company because that other company owns the majority of the shares in it.

sustainable Involving the use of natural products and energy in a way that does not harm the environment.

trademark A name, symbol or design that a company uses for its products and cannot be used by anyone else.

water harvesting Collecting rainwater and storing it so that people can use it for drinking, for animals and for watering crops.

water stewardship Managing the use of water, for example, by using as little as possible, reducing water pollution and harvesting rainwater.

Index

BIG BU$INE$$

Contents of all the titles in the series:

Apple
978 0 7502 7090 8

An Apple in every home
The origins of Apple
Building the Apple brand
Fallout at the top
Steve returns to Apple
Riding the Internet wave
Apple explores music
The invention of the iPhone
There's an app for that!
Apple takes on publishing
What makes Apple so 'must-have'?
What does the future hold for Apple?
Design your own App for the App Store!
Do you have what it takes to work at Apple?

Disney
978 0 7502 6922 3

Disney on top
The birth of Mickey Mouse
Snow White and the Seven Oscars
Disney in your living room
The birth of the theme park
Life and death at Disney
The wonderful world of Disney
Disney grows up
A store in every town
Disney Interactive
Steadying the ship
What does the future hold for Disney?
Design your own Disney venture
Do you have what it takes to work at Disney?

Microsoft
978 0 7502 6924 7

Riding high
From small beginnings
The launch of MS-DOS
Opening Windows, 1983
'A computer on every desk'
Bill Gates: the man behind Microsoft
The Internet takes off
New Windows to the world
Entering the games world: Xbox
Into the clouds
Microsoft in the community
Microsoft's vision
Develop your own Microsoft product
Do you have what it takes to work at Microsoft?

Cadbury
978 0 7502 6923 0

Sweet success
The founder: John Cadbury
Building the business 1861-1900
Philanthropy: a helping hand
Enter Dairy Milk 1900-20
Facing the competition 1920-45
Business booms 1945-69
A Cadbury world
Cadbury Schweppes 1969-89
New markets, new products 1990-2010
Purple goes green
The end of an era
Design your own Cadbury venture
Do you have what it takes to work at Cadbury?

Facebook
978 0 7502 7088 5

Birth of a new brand
Facebook Inc
The site at a glance
The idea keeps on growing
An expert on board
Making popularity pay
To high school and beyond
Going global
The secret to making money
There's more to Facebook than friends
To share or not to share?
What's next for Facebook?
Invent your own Facebook app
Do you have what it takes to work at Facebook?

Nike
978 0 7502 6925 4

Nike rules the world
The birth of the business
Growing the company
Better by design
The Nike brand is born
First hiccups
Built on innovation
Star power
Life at Nike HQ
Coming through adversity
Going global
What does the future hold for Nike?
Do you have what it takes to work at Nike?

Coca-Cola
978 0 7502 6921 6

Coca-Cola at the top
'A delicious and refreshing beverage'
Coke and the American way of life
New-look Coke - the 'real thing'
Coke and sports
New markets, new drinks
Coca-Cola controversies
Coca-Cola: a marketing miracle
The challenge of sustainability
Corporate social responsibility (CSR)
Muhtar Kent, head of Coca-Cola
'2020 Vision': Coca-Cola's future
Design your own Coca-Cola venture
Do you have what it takes to work at Coca Cola?

Google
978 0 7502 7089 2

The world gets Googled!
What makes Google so good?
Google is born
Setting up the company
Standing out from the competition
Making a profit
Keeping the staff happy
Google goes public
Expanding the business
Diversifying the business
Google changes the world
Making Google future-proof
Invent the next Google product!
Do you have what it takes to work at Google?

Nintendo
978 0 7502 7091 5

Nintendo rules the world!
Seizing the opportunity
From playing cards to electronics
Building a reputation for fun
The Game Boy arrives!
The battle for your living room
The business of games creation
Expanding the games market
Mario – the superstar for 30 years!
Games the whole family can play
Games for everyday life
Making plans for the future
Invent a new Nintendo game!
Do you have what it takes to work at Nintendo?

WAYLAND